Traditi

Wisconsin

Recipes

Introduction

Wisconsin is located in the north-central part of the United States of America near the Great Lakes. When many people think of Wisconsin they think of cheese. Specifically, they think of Wisconsin Cheddar. But Wisconsin is known as "America's Dairyland" because it is one of the nation's leading dairy producers of many different kinds of cheeses. Cheese is such an important product for residents of Wisconsin that hundreds of Packers' fans can be seen wearing foam cheese-heads whenever a Green Bay NFL football game is on television.

Wisconsin is also known for brewing beer. Milwaukee is the largest city and is one of the nation's largest producers of beers. The beer brewing influence can be tasted in much of the cuisine which features pub grub as well as beer battered faire.

Many of the early settlers of Wisconsin were German and Scandinavian. This has also influenced the state foods as bratwurst is a state favorite.

Wisconsin is an agricultural state with many crops being official state foods such as cranberries and sweet corn. This cookbook has all the traditional Wisconsin recipes using all the foods and products that are representative of this delicious Mid-West American state.

Wisconsin Bratwurst

Ingredients:

2 lbs. fresh bratwurst sausages
2 onions, thinly sliced
1 cup butter
6 (12 fluid oz.) cans or bottles beer
1 1/2 tsps. ground black pepper

Directions:

1. Prick bratwurst with fork to prevent them from exploding as they cook.
2. Place in a large stock pot with the onions, butter, and beer.
3. Place pot over medium heat, and simmer for 15 to 20 minutes.
4. Preheat grill for medium-high heat.
5. Lightly oil grate.
6. Cook bratwurst on preheated grill for 10 to 14 minutes, turning occasionally to brown evenly.
7. Serve hot off the grill with onions on hoagie rolls.

Wisconsin Beer Cheese Soup

Ingredients:

1 1/2 cups diced carrots
1 1/2 cups diced onion
1 1/2 cups diced celery
2 cloves garlic, minced
1 tsp. hot pepper sauce
1/8 tsp. cayenne pepper
1/2 tsp. salt
1/4 tsp. black pepper
3 cups chicken broth
2 cups beer
1/3 cup butter
1/3 cup flour
4 cups milk or half and half
6 cups shredded sharp Cheddar cheese
1 tbsp. Dijon mustard
2 tsps. Worcestershire sauce
1 tsp. dry mustard
Popped popcorn, for garnish

Directions:

1. In a large saucepan over medium heat, stir together carrots, onion, celery, and garlic.
2. Stir in hot pepper sauce, cayenne pepper, salt, and pepper.
3. Pour in chicken broth and beer; simmer until vegetables are tender, about 12 minutes.
4. Remove from heat.
5. Meanwhile, heat butter in a large soup pot over medium-high heat.
6. Stir in flour with a wire whisk; cook, stirring until the flour is light brown, about 3 or 4 minutes.
7. Gradually stir in milk, whisking to prevent scorching, until thickened.
8. Remove from heat, and gradually stir in cheese.
9. Keep warm.
10. Stir beer mixture into cheese mixture.
11. Stir in Dijon mustard, Worcestershire sauce, and dry mustard.
12. Adjust for hot pepper sauce.
13. Bring to a simmer, and cook 10 minutes.
14. Serve topped with popcorn.

Milwaukee Rye Bread

Ingredients:

4 potatoes - peeled, boiled and mashed
3/4 cup cornmeal
3 cups water
1 1/2 tbsps. salt
1 tbsp. white sugar
2 tbsps. shortening
1 (.6 oz.) cake compressed fresh yeast
1/4 cup warm water (110 degrees F/45 degrees C)
6 cups rye flour 2 cups whole wheat flour

Directions:

1. In a small saucepan, cover peeled potatoes with water.
2. Bring water to a boil and cook until tender, about 15 minutes.
3. Drain and mash; let cool.
4. In a separate sauce pan, stir the cornmeal into the 3 cups water.
5. Bring to a boil and cook for 2 minutes.
6. Stir in salt, sugar and shortening.
7. Let cool to lukewarm.
8. In a large bowl, dissolve yeast in warm water.
9. Add cooled cornmeal mixture and 2 cups of the cooled mashed potatoes.
10. Stir in the rye flour and whole wheat flour 1 cup at a time; beating well after each addition.
11. When the dough has pulled together, turn it out onto a lightly floured surface and knead until smooth and elastic, about 8 minutes.
12. Lightly oil a large bowl, place the dough in the bowl and turn to coat with oil.
13. Cover with a damp cloth and let rise in a warm place until doubled in volume, about 1 hour.
14. Deflate the dough and turn it out onto a lightly floured surface.
15. Divide the dough into three equal pieces and form into loaves.
16. Place the loaves into three lightly greased 9x5 inch loaf pans.
17. Cover the loaves with a damp cloth and let rise until doubled in volume, about 40 minutes.
18. Meanwhile, preheat oven to 375 degrees F (190 degrees C).
19. Bake in preheated oven for 60 to 70 minutes, until loaves sound hollow when tapped on the bottom.

Wisconsin Blue Ribbon Chili

Ingredients:

1 1/2 pounds lean ground beef
1 stalk celery, chopped
1/2 red bell pepper, chopped
1 white onion, chopped
1 (28 oz.) can diced tomatoes
1 1/2 cups tomato juice
2 cups water
2 tbsps. chili powder
2 tbsps. brown sugar
6 cubes beef bouillon
3/4 cup uncooked elbow macaroni

Directions:

1. Place ground beef into a large soup pot over medium heat.
2. Cook the beef until it begins to lose its pink color, about 8 minutes, breaking the meat up into crumbles as it cooks; stir in celery, red bell pepper, and onion.
3. Continue to cook until the beef is browned, about 8 more minutes.
4. Drain excess fat.
5. Stir in diced tomatoes, tomato juice, water, chili powder, brown sugar, and beef bouillon cubes; cover, reduce heat, and simmer for 30 minutes.
6. Stir in the macaroni, and continue simmering until the pasta is tender, 10 to 15 more minutes.

Wisconsin Brat & Beer Cheese Dip

Ingredients:

1 pound fresh bratwurst sausages, casings removed
2 tbsps. butter
1/4 cup flour
1 1/2 cups milk
1 cup Milwaukee beer
1 pkg. pork gravy mix
1 1/2 cups shredded sharp Cheddar cheese
3/4 cup cheese curds or shredded white Cheddar cheese

Directions:

1. Preheat oven to 350 degrees F.
2. Cook and crumble sausage in large skillet on medium-high heat until browned.
3. Drain fat.
4. Remove from skillet. Set aside.
5. Melt butter in same large skillet on medium heat.
6. Sprinkle with flour.
7. Cook and stir 1 minute.
8. Gradually stir in milk, beer and Gravy Mix with whisk until smooth.
9. Stirring constantly, bring to boil.
10. Reduce heat and simmer 5 minutes or until sauce starts to thicken.
11. Gradually stir in shredded cheese until melted and smooth.
12. Stir in cooked sausage. Spoon into 9-inch glass pie plate.
13. Sprinkle with cheese curds.
14. Bake 15 minutes or until cheese melts.
15. Serve with soft pretzel bites or pretzel chips.

Wisconsin Five-Cheese Bake

Ingredients:

1 (16 oz.) package elbow macaroni
1 cup shredded mozzarella cheese
1 cup shredded Swiss cheese
1 cup grated Parmesan cheese
1 cup shredded provolone cheese
1/2 cup ricotta cheese 1/2 cup sour cream
1/2 cup heavy cream 1 tbsp. chopped fresh parsley
1/2 tsp. dried Italian seasoning
1/2 tsp. garlic salt

Directions:

1. Preheat the oven to 400 degrees F (200 degrees C).
2. Lightly grease a 9x13 inch baking dish.
3. Bring a large pot of lightly salted water to a boil.
4. Add macaroni, and cook until tender, 6 to 8 minutes.
5. Drain.
6. In a large bowl, toss together the mozzarella cheese, Swiss cheese, Parmesan cheese and Provolone cheese.
7. Remove about 1/2 cup for topping and set aside.
8. In a separate bowl, stir together the ricotta cheese, sour cream and heavy cream.
9. Season with parsley, Italian seasoning and garlic salt.
10. Pour the ricotta cheese mixture and drained macaroni into the bowl with the cheeses and toss lightly.
11. Do not mix too thoroughly, it's better left messy.
12. Pour into the prepared baking dish.
13. Sprinkle the reserved cheese over the top.
14. Bake in the preheated oven until cheese is melted, about 10 minutes, then turn the oven to broil. Broil for about 5 minutes to brown the top.

Wisconsin Marinated Venison

Ingredients:

2 pounds venison (deer meat)
1/2 (10 fluid oz.) bottle Worcestershire sauce
1 (12 fluid oz.) can or bottle beer
1 1/2 cups all-purpose flour
1 tbsp. onion salt
1 tbsp. garlic powder vegetable oil for frying

Directions:

1. Pound venison flat, and cut into 1 inch strips; place in a large bowl.
2. Pour in Worcestershire sauce and beer.
3. Cover, and refrigerate for 1 hour or more.
4. In a shallow bowl, combine flour, onion salt and garlic powder.
5. Drag soaked meat through the flour mixture.
6. Heat oil in a large heavy skillet, and fry meat until golden brown.

Milwaukee Beer Batter

Ingredients:

1 cup all-purpose flour
1 egg, beaten
1 tsp. garlic powder
1/2 tsp. ground black pepper
1 1/2 cups beer

Directions:

1. In a small mixing bowl add flour, egg, garlic powder, and black pepper.
2. Stir in 1 cup or more of beer for desired texture.

Green Bay Smoked Fish Dip

Ingredients:

2 cups flaked smoked whitefish
2 tbsps. mayonnaise
4 tbsps. sour cream
1 pinch Old Bay seasoning
4 drops hot pepper sauce, or to taste
3 drops Worcestershire sauce, or to taste
3 drops liquid smoke flavoring (optional)
Pepper to taste

Directions:

1. Place whitefish, mayonnaise, and sour cream in the bowl of a food processor.
2. Season with Old Bay (Tm) seasoning, hot pepper sauce, Worcestershire sauce, liquid smoke, and cracked black pepper.
3. Blend all ingredients until consistency reaches a spread.

Green Bay Crispy Fried Fish

Ingredients:

1 egg
1 1/2 cups beer
1 cup all-purpose flour
1 tsp. garlic powder
1/2 tsp. salt
1/2 tsp. ground black pepper
1 pound cod fillets
2 cups crushed cornflake crumbs
1 tsp. Cajun seasoning
1 quart oil for frying

Directions:

1. In a medium bowl, beat together egg, beer, flour, garlic powder, salt, and pepper.
2. Place cod in the bowl, and thoroughly coat with the mixture.
3. In a separate medium bowl, mix the cornflake crumbs and Cajun seasoning.
4. Dip the cod in the crumb mixture, and thoroughly coat all sides.
5. In a large, heavy skillet or deep fryer, heat the oil to 365 degrees F (185 degrees C).
6. Fry the fish until golden brown, and flesh is easily flaked with a fork.

Green Bay Nutty Coconut Fish

Ingredients:

1/4 cup mayonnaise
1/4 cup prepared brown mustard
1/2 cup dry bread crumbs
1/4 cup shredded coconut
1/4 cup chopped mixed nuts
1 tsp. granulated sugar
1 tsp. salt
1/2 tsp. cayenne pepper
1 lb. whitefish fillets

Directions:

1. Preheat oven to 375 degrees F (190 degrees C).
2. Lightly grease a medium baking dish.
3. In a small bowl, blend mayonnaise and brown mustard.
4. In a medium bowl, mix dry bread crumbs, shredded coconut, chopped mixed nuts, sugar, salt, and cayenne pepper.
5. Dip fish in the mayonnaise mixture, then in the bread crumb mixture.
6. Arrange coated fish fillets in the prepared baking dish.
7. Bake 20 minutes in the preheated oven, until fish is easily flaked with a fork.

Milwaukee Beer Dip

Ingredients:

2 (8 oz.) pkgs. cream cheese, softened
1 (1 oz.) pkg. dry Ranch-style dressing mix
1 (12 fluid oz.) can or bottle beer

Directions:

1. In a medium bowl, mix the cream cheese, dry ranch-style dressing mix and beer until well blended and creamy.
2. Serve and enjoy!

Milwaukee Apple Banana Cupcakes

Ingredients:

2 cups all-purpose flour
1 tsp. baking soda
1 tsp. salt
1/2 tsp. ground cinnamon
1/2 tsp. ground nutmeg
2/3 cup shortening
1 1/4 cups white sugar
2 eggs
1 tsp. vanilla extract
1/4 cup buttermilk
1 cup ripe bananas, mashed
2 apples, peeled, cored and shredded

Directions:

1. Preheat oven to 375 degrees F (190 degrees C).
2. Grease and flour 24 muffin cups, or use paper liners.
3. Sift together the flour, baking soda, salt, cinnamon, and nutmeg.
4. Set aside.
5. In a large bowl, cream together the shortening and sugar until light and fluffy.
6. Beat in the eggs one at a time, then stir in the vanilla and buttermilk.
7. Beat in the flour mixture, mixing just until incorporated.
8. Fold in the mashed bananas and shredded apples.
9. Fill each muffin cup half full.
10. Bake in the preheated oven for 20 to 25 minutes, or until a toothpick inserted into the center comes out clean. Allow to cool.

Milwaukee Dogs

Ingredients:

1 tbsp. vegetable oil
1 med. onion, sliced
1 pkg. (16 oz.) beer bratwurst (6 count)
6 slices Swiss cheese
6 rye or whole wheat hot dog buns, split, toasted
1/2 cup sauerkraut
2 tbsps. coarse-grained mustard

Directions:

1. In 10-inch nonstick skillet, heat oil over medium-low heat until hot.
2. Cook onion in oil 20 to 25 minutes, stirring occasionally, until brown and softened.
1. Heat gas or charcoal grill.
2. Place bratwurst on grill over medium heat.
3. Cook uncovered 10 to 15 minutes, turning frequently, until hot.
4. Wrap each bratwurst with slice of cheese; place on buns.
5. Top with sauerkraut, onion and mustard.

Milwaukee Beer Battered Grilled Cheese Sandwiches

Ingredients:

6 slices hickory-smoked bacon
4 slices rustic white bread
2 slices provolone cheese (3/4 oz. each)
2 slices Cheddar cheese (3/4 oz. each)
1 egg
3/4 cup pale ale beer
1/4 cup all-purpose flour
1/4 tsp. chipotle chili powder
1 tbsp. butter

Directions:

1. In 12-inch nonstick skillet, cook bacon until crisp; drain on paper towel.
2. On 2 of the bread slices, place 1 slice provolone cheese, 3 slices bacon and 1 slice Cheddar cheese on each. Top with remaining bread slices.
3. Heat griddle or skillet over medium-high heat or to 375 degrees F.
4. In shallow bowl, beat egg, beer, flour and chili powder with fork until smooth.
5. Dip each sandwich into batter, giving it a few seconds on each side to absorb the batter; drain excess batter back into bowl.
6. Melt butter on hot griddle.
7. Place sandwiches on griddle.
8. Cook 3 to 4 minutes on each side until golden brown.

Milwaukee Moussaka

Ingredients:

2 medium eggplants, peeled
1/4 tsp. salt, or to taste
4 oz. bacon, diced
2 onions, sliced
1/2 green bell pepper, chopped
1 (28 oz.) can peeled and diced tomatoes, drained
1/8 tsp. black pepper
1/4 tsp. dried thyme
1/4 tsp. dried marjoram 1 pinch garlic powder
1/2 tsp. dried sage 2 tbsps. olive oil
8 oz. shredded Swiss cheese grated Parmesan cheese

Directions:

1. Slice eggplant lengthwise into 1/2 inch slices.
2. Place slices into a colander and sprinkle with salt.
3. Set the colander in the sink to drain off liquid.
4. Cook bacon in a skillet over medium heat until evenly browned.
5. Drain off excess grease.
6. Add onion and green pepper to the skillet, and cook until tender.
7. Stir in the tomatoes, and season with salt, pepper, thyme, marjoram, garlic powder and sage.
8. Reduce heat to medium-low and let simmer for about 10 minutes.
9. Preheat the oven to 350 degrees F (175 degrees C).
10. Heat oil in a large skillet over medium-high heat. Squeeze excess moisture from the eggplant.
11. Fry the eggplant slices in the hot oil until browned on both sides.
12. Arrange half of the eggplant slices in the bottom of a 1 1/2 quart baking dish. Top with half of the bacon and tomato mixture.
13. Sprinkle with half of the Swiss cheese.
14. Repeat layers ending with cheese on top.
15. Bake, uncovered, for 35 to 45 minutes in the preheated oven.
16. Let stand for 15 minutes before serving.
17. Top with grated Parmesan cheese.

Wisconsin Beer-Brined Chicken Drummies

Brine and Chicken Ingredients:

2 cups water
2 tbsps. kosher (coarse) salt
2 tbsps. packed brown sugar
2 cans or bottles (12 oz. each) beer, chilled
24 chicken wing drummettes (3 lbs.)

Rub Ingredients:

3 tbsps. packed brown sugar
3 tsps. salt
2 tsps. garlic powder
3/4 tsp. pepper
2 tbsps. vegetable oil

Directions:

1. In 1-gallon resealable food-storage plastic bag, mix water, 2 tbsps. kosher salt, 2 tbsps. brown sugar and the beer.
2. Add drummettes. Seal bag; place in large bowl.
3. Refrigerate at least 8 hours but no longer than 24 hours.
4. Heat oven to 375F degrees F. Line 15x10x1-inch pan with foil.
5. Remove chicken from brine; discard brine.
6. Rinse chicken thoroughly with cool water and pat dry with paper towels.
7. Place chicken in pan.
8. In small bowl, mix 3 tbsps. brown sugar, 3 tsps. salt, the garlic powder and pepper. Brush oil over chicken.
9. Sprinkle with rub mixture.
10. Bake uncovered 45 to 55 minutes, turning after 25 minutes, or until chicken is no longer pink in center.

Wisconsin Grilled Beer-Brined Chicken

Brine and Chicken Ingredients:

2 cups water
1/4 cup kosher (coarse) salt
1/4 cup packed brown sugar
4 cans or bottles (12 oz. each) beer or nonalcoholic beer, chilled
2 cut-up whole chickens (3 to 3 1/2 lb. each)

Barbecue Rub Ingredients:

1 tbsp. paprika
1 tsp. table salt
1/2 tsp. onion powder
1/2 tsp. garlic powder
1/2 tsp. pepper
1/4 cup vegetable oil

Directions:

1. In 6- to 8-quart noncorrosive (stainless steel, enamel-coated or plastic) container or stockpot, mix water, kosher salt and brown sugar, stirring until salt and sugar are dissolved.
2. Stir in beer.
3. Add chicken.
4. Cover; refrigerate at least 8 hours but no longer than 24 hours.
5. Line 15x10-inch pan with sides with foil.
6. Remove chicken from brine; rinse thoroughly under cool running water and pat dry with paper towels. Discard brine.
7. Place chicken in pan.
8. Refrigerate uncovered 1 hour to dry chicken skin.
9. Meanwhile, in small bowl, mix all rub ingredients except oil; set aside.
10. Heat gas or charcoal grill for indirect cooking. Brush oil over chicken; sprinkle rub mixture over chicken.
11. For two-burner gas grill, heat one burner to medium.
12. Place chicken on unheated side. For one-burner gas grill, place chicken on grill over low heat. For charcoal grill, move medium coals to edge of firebox; place chicken over drip pan.
13. Cover grill; cook 15 minutes.

14. Turn chicken over; cover grill and cook 20 to 30 minutes longer, turning occasionally, until juice of chicken is clear when thickest piece is cut to bone (170 degrees F for breasts; 180 degrees F for thighs and drumsticks).

Wisconsin Grilled Beer-Marinated Rump Roast

Ingredients:

2 tbsps. vegetable oil
1 med. onion, chopped (1/2 cup)
1 clove garlic, finely chopped
1/2 cup chili sauce
1/2 tsp. salt
1/4 tsp. pepper
1 can or bottle (12 oz.) beer
3 1/2- to 4-pound rolled beef rump roast
2 cups hickory wood chips

Directions:

1. In 1-quart saucepan, heat oil over medium-high heat.
2. Cook onion and garlic in oil, stirring frequently, until onion is tender; remove from heat.
3. Stir in chili sauce, salt, pepper and beer.
4. Place beef in shallow glass or plastic dish or re-sealable food-storage plastic bag.
5. Pour beer mixture over beef; turn beef to coat with marinade.
6. Cover dish or seal bag and refrigerate, turning beef occasionally, at least 8 hours but no longer than 24 hours.
7. Cover wood chips with water; soak 30 minutes. If using charcoal grill, place drip pan directly under grilling area, and arrange coals around edge of firebox. Heat coals or gas grill for indirect heat.
8. Remove beef from marinade; reserve marinade. Insert spit rod lengthwise through center of beef.
9. Hold firmly in place with adjustable holding forks. Insert barbecue meat thermometer so tip is near center of beef but not touching spit rod.
10. Drain wood chips.
11. Add about 1/2 cup wood chips to medium-low coals or lava rock.
12. Cover and grill beef on rotisserie over drip pan and 4 inches from medium-low heat about 2 hours for medium doneness (160 degrees F), brushing occasionally with marinade and adding 1/2 cup wood chips to coals or rock every 30 minutes.
13. Remove spit rod, holding forks and thermometer. Discard any remaining marinade.

14. Cover beef with foil and let stand 15 minutes before slicing.

Grilled Backyard Beer Burgers

Ingredients:

1 1/2 lb. lean (at least 80%) ground beef
1 small onion, finely chopped (1/4 cup)
1/4 cup beer
1 tbsp. Worcestershire sauce
1 tsp. salt
1/4 tsp. pepper
2 cloves garlic, finely chopped
6 rye or whole wheat hamburger buns, split
Ketchup, if desired
Pickle planks, if desired

Directions:

1. Heat gas or charcoal grill. In medium bowl, mix all ingredients except buns, ketchup and pickles. Shape mixture into 6 patties, about 3/4 inch thick.
2. Place patties on grill rack over medium heat.
3. Cover grill; cook 10 to 15 minutes, turning once, until meat thermometer inserted in center of patties reads 160°F.
4. Add buns, cut sides down, for last 4 minutes of grilling or until toasted.
5. Top burgers with ketchup and pickle planks; serve on buns.

Green Bay Potatoes

Ingredients:

1 lg. pkg. frozen hash brown pieces
1 (16 oz.) container sour cream
1 sm. can cream of mushroom soup
1 1/2 or 2 cup shredded sharp Cheddar cheese
Salt and pepper to taste
1/2 stick butter, melted
2 cup crushed corn flakes

Directions:

1. Mix all except corn flakes.
2. Place in roasting pan sprayed with Pam.
3. Bake at 350 degrees for 1 1/2 hours.
4. Covered for 45 minutes then cover with crushed corn flakes and bake remaining 1/2 hour to 45 minutes leaving lid off.

Wisconsin Pudding

Ingredients:

1 cup flour
1/2 cup butter, softened
1/2 cup nuts, chopped
8 pkg. (8 oz.) cream cheese
1 cup confectioners sugar
1 container whipped topping
1 pkg. (6 oz.) instant chocolate pudding
2 1/2 cup milk
Chocolate bar or nuts (for topping)

Directions:

1. First Layer: Mix 1 cup flour, 1/2 cup softened butter and 1/2 cup chopped nuts. Press into 9x13 inch pan and bake 10 minutes at 400 degrees F. Cool.
2. Second Layer: Soften 8 oz. pkg. of cream cheese.
3. Mix with 1 cup confectioners sugar and 1 cup whipped topping.
4. Third Layer: One 6 oz. instant chocolate pudding made with 2 1/2 cups milk.
5. Pour over cream cheese layer.
6. Fourth Layer: Top with remaining whipped topping and shaved chocolate bar or crushed nuts.

Wisconsin Holiday Fondue

Ingredients:

1 med. onion, chopped
1/2 lb. ground beef
2 cans (10 1/2 oz. each) pizza sauce
1 1/2 tsp. fennel seed
1 1/2 tsp. leaf oregano
1/4 tsp. garlic powder
2 1/2 cup (10 oz.) shredded Wisconsin Cheddar cheese
1 cup (4 oz.) shredded Wisconsin Mozzarella cheese

Directions:

1. In a saucepan over medium heat, brown onion and ground beef.
2. Drain.
3. Add pizza sauce and seasonings, stir until heated.
4. Add cheese by the handfuls, stir until smooth.
5. Pour into fondue pot. Keep warm while serving.
6. Serve with Italian or French bread cut into pieces, or over toasted English muffins for luncheon treat.

Wisconsin Harvest Delight Soup

Ingredients:

1 ring bologna, cut into 1 inch chunks
1 (28 oz.) can diced tomatoes
1 (15 oz.) can peas and carrots
1 (11 oz.) can mandarin oranges
1 (15 oz.) can diced rutabagas
2 or 3 slices tomato-basil cheddar cheese
1 tsp. sea salt
2 tsps. parsley flakes

Directions:

1. You're going to like this! When you set down and start eating your soup, eat a chunk of tomato basil cheddar cheese with it.
2. Start by cutting slicing the ring bologna into one-inch cuts.
3. Add them to a big pot.
4. Then add tomatoes, peas and carrots, mandarin oranges, diced rutabagas, sea salt, and parsley flakes.
5. Simmer over medium-low heat for at least 30 minutes.
6. Taste and adjust seasoning.
7. Enjoy it with your tomato-basil cheddar cheese on the side!

Wisconsin Apple Crisp

Ingredients:

8 sm. apples (4-6 med.)
Sprinkle of cinnamon
3/4 cup oatmeal
3/4 cup brown sugar
1/2 cup flour
1 stick butter

Directions:

1. Mix together oatmeal, brown sugar, flour, and butter for crumb topping.
2. Place apples in 9x13 inch pan.
3. Sprinkle cinnamon on top.
4. Sprinkle crumb topping over all.
5. Bake at 350 degrees for 35-40 minutes.

Wisconsin Apple Cake

Ingredients:

2 cup peeled, diced apples
1 cup sugar
1 egg, beaten
1/4 tsp. salt
1 1/2 tsp. cinnamon
1/2 cup chopped nuts
1 tsp. soda
1 cup flour
Mix apples and sugar; let stand for at least 1 hour until sugar has dissolved, stirring frequently.
Add eggs, salt, cinnamon and nuts; mix.
Stir together soda and flour, stir into apple mixture.
Pour into well greased 9 inch square pan.
Bake at 350 degrees for 40 to 45 minutes. Do not remove from pan.

SAUCE Directions:

1. While cake is baking mix together: 1/2 cup white sugar 2 tbsp. flour
2. 1 cup water 1/4 cup butter 1 tsp. vanilla
3. Mix sugars and flour; stir in water, butter and vanilla. Boil 2 minutes, stirring constantly.
4. Pour hot sauce over cake that is still in pan.
5. Serve warm or cold with whipped cream or hard sauce.

Wisconsin Apple Torte

Ingredients:

1/2 cup butter, softened
1/3 cup sugar
1/4 tsp. vanilla
1 cup whole wheat flour
1 (8 oz.) pkg. cream cheese, softened
1/4 cup sugar
1 egg
1 tsp. vanilla
1/3 cup sugar
1/4 tsp. cinnamon
1/4 tsp. nutmeg
2 cup sliced, peeled apples (macs or duchess)
Half white and half brown sugar.

Directions:

1. Cream butter and sugar, stir in vanilla, then flour. Press the mixture into the bottom of a 9" springform pan.
2. In a separate bowl, mix cream cheese, sugar, egg and vanilla.
3. Pour this mixture over the crust.
4. Mix the sugar, cinnamon and nutmeg.
5. Add apple slices as they are cut up.
6. Arrange apple slices on top of the filling.
7. Bake at 425 degrees for 10 minutes, then at 375 degrees for 25 minutes.
8. Remove from oven and pour the leftover apple juices on top of the torte. Cool before removing the springform.

Wisconsin Chicken Soup

Ingredients:

1 chicken, boiled and de-boned (reserve broth)
3 sliced carrots
1 chopped onion
1 bell pepper, chopped
2 bay leaves
1 clove garlic
3 whole cloves

Directions:

1. Cook vegetables and spices in chicken broth until done. Lift out spices.
2. Add chicken and bring to a boil.
3. Serve hot over rice.

Wisconsin Birthday Cake

Ingredients:

1/2 cup butter
2 cup sugar
4 eggs
3 cup flour
1/2 tsp. baking powder
1/2 tsp. baking soda
1/2 tsp. salt

Directions:

1. Cut up one small bottle of Maraschino cherries.
2. Cut up 1 cup nuts. Put cherry juice in cup and fill up to 1 cup with milk.
3. Mix and pour into Bundt pan.
4. Bake at 325 degrees for 1 hour.

Wisconsin Butter Balls

Ingredients:

1 cup butter
2 1/4 cup flour
1/4 tsp. salt
3/4 cup chopped nutmeats
1/2 cup confectioners' sugar
1 tsp. vanilla

Directions:

1. Mix, form into balls.
2. Bake at 300 degrees for 25 to 30 minutes, while hot roll in powdered sugar.
3. Cool and roll again.

Wisconsin Three Cheese Chicken Bake

Ingredients:

1/3 cup chopped onion
3 tbsp. butter
1/3 cup milk
1/4 cup chopped pimiento
1/2 tsp. basil
6 oz. sliced mushrooms
3 cup chopped chicken
1 1/2 cup creamed cottage cheese
2 cup grated cheddar cheese
1/2 cup Parmesan cheese
1/2 cup chopped pepper
1 can cream of chicken soup
1 (8 oz.) pkg. Kluski noodles

Directions:

1. Saute onion and green peppers in butter; stir in soup, milk, mushrooms, pimiento and basil.
2. Place 1/2 of noodles in a 9"x13" pan.
3. Add 1/2 cottage cheese, 1/2 chicken, 1/2 cheddar cheese and Parmesan cheese in layers; repeat.
4. Cover with mushroom sauce.
5. Bake at 350 degrees for 45 minutes.
6. Top with bread crumbs, last 15 minutes. 8 to 10 servings.

Wisconsin Cheddar Chowder

Ingredients:

2 cup diced potatoes
1 cup sliced carrots
1 cup sliced celery
1/4 cup chopped onion
1 1/2 tsp. salt
1/4 tsp. pepper
1/4 cup butter
1/4 cup flour
2 cup milk
2 cup (8 oz.) shredded sharp cheddar cheese
1 cup cubed, cooked ham

Directions:

1. Add water to vegetables, just to cover.
2. Add salt and pepper, cover and simmer 10 minutes (or a little longer for softer vegetables).
3. Make white sauce with butter, flour, and milk.
4. Add cheese and stir until melted.
5. Add ham and undrained vegetables.
6. Heat, but do not boil.

Wisconsin Cheese Cake

Ingredients:

1 lb. bag marshmallows
1 cup milk
3 (8 oz.) pkgs. cream cheese
1 lg. (10 oz.) whipped topping
1 lg. (16 oz.) can crushed pineapple, drained
1 lg. box frozen strawberries, drained

Crust Ingredients:

2 cup graham cracker crumbs
1 stick butter
1 tbsp. sugar

Directions:

1. Make crust. Press into bottom of 13"x9"x2" pan. In large pan, combine milk and marshmallows.
2. Cook on low, stirring constantly until marshmallows are melted.
3. Mix cream cheese until smooth.
4. Add to marshmallow mixture. Fold in whipped topping and crushed pineapple.
5. Top with strawberries.
6. Refrigerate 4 hours or overnight.

Wisconsin Fish Chowder

Ingredients:

2 to 4 slices bacon, in 1 inch pieces
1 1/2 cup potatoes, peeled & diced
1/3 cup onion, diced
1/2 tsp. salt
1/8 tsp. pepper
1/2 cup water
1 lb. pike or perch
3 cup milk
1 tbsp. fresh parsley, chopped

Directions:

1. Fry the bacon until golden brown.
2. Add the potatoes, onions, salt, pepper and water.
3. Cover and cook over moderate heat 5 to 10 minutes.
4. Add the boned and cut up fish.
5. Cover and continue cooking until potatoes are done, about 10 to 12 minutes.
6. Add the milk and heat through.
7. Add the parsley.

Wisconsin Dairy Punch

Ingredients:

1 qt. white soda or 7-Up
1 qt. milk
1 qt. sherbet, any flavor
Maraschino cherries

Directions:

1. Pour soda and milk into punch bowl.
2. Scoop in sherbet.
3. Mix with large spoon until sherbet is partly blended.
4. Garnish with maraschino cherries.

Wisconsin Cranberry Salad

Ingredients:

1 cup fresh cranberries
1 cup tart apples
1 cup sugar
1/2 cup pecans, chopped
1 cup whipped topping

Directions:

1. Combine apples, sugar and cranberries in a large bowl.
2. Cover and chill for 24 hours.
3. On the next day, add pecans and whipped topping
4. Add to a food processor.
5. Mix again and put back in the refrigerator to chill.
6. Serve and enjoy.

Wisconsin Hot Beef Sandwich

3-4 lb. beef roast
1 can beer
1 shot brandy
1 can cream of onion soup
1 can beef broth
Buns for serving

Directions:

1. Combine all ingredients in a roasting pan.
2. Roast at 300 degrees until beef shreds with a fork (about 4-6 hours).
3. Remove beef and shred.
4. Serve on buns.

Wisconsin Chocolate Almond Pie

1 (12 oz.) lg. milk chocolate bar with almonds
18 lg. marshmallows
1/2 cup milk
2 cup whipped cream or whipped topping
9" baked pie crust

Directions:

1. Melt candy, marshmallow and milk together. Cool.
2. Fold in 1 cup of whipped cream or whipped topping.
3. Pour mixture into baked pie shell. Chill well.
4. Top with remaining cup of whipped cream.
5. Can decorate with toasted almonds or chocolate peels.

Wisconsin Chunky Tomato Cheese Pie

5 med.-sized (1 2/3 lbs.) tomatoes
Pastry for 9-inch pie shell
2 cup cheddar cheese cubes
1/2 cup Italian-style bread crumbs
2 tbsp. flour
1 tbsp. sugar
2 tsp. salt
1/2 cup thin slices cheddar cheese

Directions:

1. Use tomatoes held at room temperature until fully ripe.
2. Cut and peel 4 tomatoes into cubes (makes about 4 cups) and slice remaining 1 tomato; set aside.
3. Preheat oven to 375 degrees.
4. On a lightly floured board roll out pastry. Fit into a 9 inch pie plate; flute edges and set aside.
5. In a large bowl combine tomato cubes, cheese, bread crumbs, flour, sugar and salt.
6. Toss until well mixed.
7. Pour into reserved pie shell.
8. Bake until cheese is melted and tomato cubes are soft, about 30 minutes.
9. Remove from oven; garnish with reserved tomato slices and cheese slices.
10. Return to oven and bake for 10 minutes or until cheese is melted and tomato slices are soft.

Wisconsin Chicken Booyah

Ingredients:

1 (4 lbs.) whole chicken, cut into pieces
2 1/2 lbs. cubed beef stew meat
1 1/2 lbs. pork shoulder roast
7 cups water
3 cups chicken broth
3 cloves garlic, whole
2 bay leaves water to cover
1 tbsp. vegetable oil
2 cups diced onion
2 cups diced carrots
2 stalks celery, diced
1 clove garlic, minced
6 potatoes, unpeeled and diced
1 1/2 cups fresh green beans, cut into 1 inch pieces
1 (14.5 oz.) can whole peeled tomatoes, drained
1 1/2 tsps. salt
1 tsp. dried rosemary
1/2 tsp. ground black pepper
1/2 tsp. dried thyme
1/2 cup frozen green peas
1 1/2 tsps. grated lemon zest
1/2 tsp. crushed red pepper
1/2 cup chopped fresh parsley, for garnish

Directions:

1. Combine the chicken, beef, pork, water and broth in a large pot and bring to a boil.
2. Add whole cloves of garlic and bay leaves, then reduce heat to low, cover and simmer for 2 hours.
3. Remove chicken, beef and pork.
4. Strip meats from bones and cut into bite size pieces.
5. Strain stock in pot and add water to yield 8 cups of stock.
6. Return meats to broth.
7. Heat oil in a medium skillet and saute the onion, carrot, celery and minced garlic for about 5 minutes.
8. Add saute mixture to pot along with the potatoes, beans, tomatoes, salt, rosemary, pepper and thyme.

9. Bring to a boil, reduce heat to low and simmer uncovered for about 10 minutes.
10. Stir in the peas, lemon zest and red pepper.
11. Heat through and serve garnished with parsley.

Wisconsin Butter Burgers

Ingredients:

1 stick plus 6 tbsps. unsalted butter, at room temperature
2 onions, chopped
Kosher salt
Freshly ground pepper
1 lb. ground beef sirloin
6 soft hamburger buns, split

Directions:

1. Preheat the broiler.
2. Melt 2 tbsps. butter in a large cast-iron skillet over medium heat.
3. Add the onions and cook until translucent, 6 to 8 minutes.
4. Add 1/3 cup water, cover and continue cooking until the onions are golden brown, about 15 more minutes.
5. Season with salt and pepper.
6. Transfer the onions to a bowl and wipe out the skillet.
7. Divide the meat into 6 loose balls, then gently flatten into thin patties. Heat the skillet over high heat.
8. Add the patties to the hot skillet, smash them flat with a spatula and season with salt and pepper.
9. Cook, flipping once, until well done, about 3 minutes per side.
10. Meanwhile, toast the buns under the broiler.
11. Put the patties on the bottom buns and top each with 1/4 cup sauteed onions. Smear 2 tbsps. butter on the cut side of each top bun, then put on top of the burgers.
12. Slice in half and serve immediately.

Wisconsin Cranberry Bliss Cookies

Cookies Ingredients:

3 cups flour
1 tsp. baking soda
1 tsp. salt
1 cup (2 sticks) butter, softened
1 cup granulated sugar
1 cup packed brown sugar
2 eggs
2 tsp. vanilla extract, store-bought or homemade
1 cup white chocolate chips
1 cup dried cranberries

Frosting Ingredients:

1 (8 oz.) bar cream cheese, room temperature
1/2 cup white chocolate chips, melted in the microwave or double-boiler
1 tsp. vanilla extract, store-bought or homemade
2 cups powdered sugar

Topping Ingredients:

1 cup dried cranberries, roughly chopped
1/4 cup white chocolate chips, melted in the microwave or double-boiler

Cookies Directions:

1. Preheat oven to 350 degrees F (175 degrees C).
2. In a separate bowl, whisk together flour, baking soda and salt until well-blended.
3. Set aside.
4. Using an electric mixer on medium-high speed, beat the butter and sugars together until light and fluffy, about 2 minutes.
5. Add in the eggs one at a time, beating in between to incorporate.
6. Add the vanilla, then reduce the speed to low, and slowly add in the dry ingredients. Increase the speed to medium, and continue beating until well-combined.
7. Fold in the white chocolate chips and cranberries, and mix until just-combined. (Do not overmix.)

8. Cover and refrigerate dough for at least 1 hour. Then place dough by rounded tbsp.-fulls onto a baking sheet that has been prepared with parchment paper, at least 2.5-inches apart.
9. Bake for 10-12 minutes, or until the cookies are lightly golden around the edges.
10. Remove pan, and transfer the cookies to a cooling rack until cool.
11. Repeat with remaining dough until all cookies are baked.
12. Wait until cookies reach room temperature before adding frosting and toppings.

Frosting Directions:

1. Using an electric mixer on medium speed, beat together the cream cheese and melted white chocolate until combined. (Be sure that your cream cheese really is at room temperature before adding the white chocolate. Otherwise the chocolate could seize up.)
2. Add in the vanilla and mix until combined.
3. Then reduce speed to low and add the powdered sugar.
4. Mix until incorporated. Then use a rubber spatula to scrape down the sides of the bowl, and beat once more for 1 minute on medium speed until the frosting is smooth.
5. Add more powdered sugar for a thicker frosting if you like.
6. Spread the frosting on the cooled cookies.
7. Immediately sprinkle the frosted cookies with the chopped dried cranberries.
8. Use a fork to drizzle on the frosting, swishing it back and forth over the cookies.

Wisconsin Homemade Cranberry Sauce

1 bag (12 oz. bag) cranberries
1 cup cranberry juice
1 cup pure maple syrup
3 tbsps. orange juice

Directions:

1. Wash bag of cranberries under cool water, then dump into a medium saucepan.
2. Pour in 1 cup of cranberry juice.
3. Pour in 1 cup maple syrup.
4. Add orange juice.
5. Stir together and turn heat on high until it reaches a boil.
6. Once it comes to a rolling boil, turn the heat down to medium low and continue cooking over lower heat for about 10 minutes, or until the juice is thick.
7. Turn off the heat.

Wisconsin Cranberry Pistachio White Chocolate Bark

Ingredients:

1 lb. white chocolate
½ cup shelled pistachios
½ cup dried cranberries

Directions:

1. Line a baking sheet with parchment paper and set aside.
2. Melt the white chocolate over a double boiler (or in 30-second intervals in the microwave on 50% power, stirring after each).
3. Once the chocolate is melted, remove from the heat and let sit for a few minutes to cool slightly, stirring occasionally.
4. Add the pistachios and cranberries and stir to combine.
5. Spread the chocolate mixture onto the prepared pan in an even layer.
6. Depending on the size of the pan and how thick you'd like your bark, you may not need the entire surface of the pan.
7. Refrigerate for at least 30 minutes, or until set.
8. Using a sharp knife, cut the bark into pieces.
9. Store in an airtight container in the refrigerator.

Wisconsin Orange-Glazed Cranberry Bread

Cranberry Orange Bread Ingredients:

2 cups Bob's Red Mill Organic Unbleached All Purpose White Flour
1 cup + 2 tbs granulated sugar, DIVIDED
1 tsp baking soda
1/4 tsp salt
zest of one orange, about one tbsp.
2 cups cranberries, chopped in half
3/4 cup buttermilk
1/4 cup freshly squeezed orange juice
1/3 cup vegetable oil
1 egg
1 tsp vanilla extract
Orange Glaze
1 cup confectioner's sugar
2-4 tbs freshly squeezed orange juice
1 tbs unsalted butter, melted
1/2 tsp vanilla extract

Directions:

1. Preheat oven to 350 degrees F.
2. Grease and flour a 9x5 loaf pan very well. Set aside.
3. Chop cranberries in half and toss with 2 tbsps. of sugar. Set aside.
4. In a large bowl, whisk flour, remaining one cup of sugar, baking soda and salt together. Fold in cranberries.
5. Make a well in the center and add buttermilk, orange juice, oil, egg and vanilla.
6. Gently stir until fully combined.
7. Pour batter into prepared loaf pan and bake for 50-60 minutes or until a toothpick inserted in the center comes out clean. When bread is taken out of oven, release the edges with a butter knife immediately to prevent any sticking. Allow bread to cool for 10 minutes in pan before inverting on a wire rack to finish cooling.
8. While bread is cooling, prepare glaze.
9. In a medium bowl, whisk confectioner's sugar, orange juice, melted butter and vanilla until smooth.
10. Add more or less orange juice for a thinner or thicker glaze.
11. Pour over cooled bread.

Wisconsin Danish Kringle

Kringle Ingredients:

3/4 cup butter
1 package dry yeast
1/4 cup lukewarm water
1/4 cup lukewarm milk
1/4 cup sugar
1/2 tsp. salt
1/2 tsp. lemon extract
1 egg
2 cups sifted all-purpose flour

Butterscotch Filling Ingredients:

1 cup brown sugar
1/3 cup butter
Pinch salt
Pinch cinnamon
1 to 2 egg whites
Fruit, nuts, raisins or jam, of choice

Directions:

1. Soften butter with a potato masher or something similar.
2. Spread the butter on waxed paper to an 8 by 16-inch rectangle. Chill.
3. Dissolve yeast in the warm water.
4. Add milk, sugar, salt, lemon extract, and egg and mix well.
5. Add flour and mix smooth by hand. A nice dough should be formed Wrap with plastic wrap and chill.
6. Roll the dough on well-floured board to an 8 by 12-inch rectangle.
7. Divide the prepared butter layer into 2 equal parts.
8. Place 1 piece of the butter on 2/3 of the dough. Fold the uncovered third of dough over the middle third (on top 1/2 of the butter layer), then fold the remaining third over the top. Chill.
9. Roll dough again to an 8 by 12-inch rectangle.
10. Place the remaining piece of chilled butter on 2/3 of the dough. Fold in the same method as the first piece of butter.
11. Gently roll dough to an 8 by 16-inch rectangle being careful not to break the layering of butter. Fold like above in thirds. This make 24 layers of butter. Chill.
12. Cut the dough into 2 equal pieces.

13. Lightly and patiently roll 1 piece at a time, until piece is about 6 by 20 inches.

Filling Directions:

14. Mix ingredient until smooth.
15. Spread center third of dough with butterscotch filling, then add fruit, nuts, raisins or jam.
16. Fold 1 of the long edges to the middle, moisten other edge and fold over top to cover filling. Seal well.
17. Put kringle on lightly greased baking sheet and form into oval shape, pressing ends of kringle together to form a continuous oval.
18. Flatten entire oval with hands.
19. Cover kringle for 1 hour at room temperature.
20. Preheat the oven to 350 degrees F.
21. Bake for about 20 to 25 minutes, until golden brown color.
22. Cool, then ice with mixture of powder sugar and water.
23. Please note that the best quality kringle require patience.
24. This process is most successful when spread out over three days.
25. Day 1, roll in first piece of butter.
26. Day 2, roll in second piece of butter and additional fold.
27. Day 3, create your kringle or other fine Danish pastries.

Wisconsin Grilled Beef Filet over Feta Creamed Corn

Ingredients:

3 tbsps. olive oil, divided
3/4 cup red onions, diced
2 garlic cloves, minced
3 1/3 cups (16 oz.) frozen corn, thawed
1 tbsp. fresh rosemary leaves, chopped
3/4 cup chicken stock
1/2 cup heavy cream
1 1/2 cups (8 oz.) Wisconsin feta cheese, crumbled
2 tbsps. butter
6 (6 oz.) beef tenderloin filets
Sea salt, to taste
Pepper, to taste
Additional Wisconsin feta cheese for garnish

Directions:

1. In a saucepan, heat 1 tbsp. oil over medium high heat; add onions and garlic; sauté 2 to 3 minutes.
2. Add corn, rosemary and chicken stock; bring to a simmer, about 7 to 10 minutes.
3. Add heavy cream and bring to a simmer.
4. Turn off heat, stir in feta and butter.
5. Continue to stir until melted; keep warm.
6. Meanwhile, rub the filets with 2 tbsps. of olive oil.
7. Season each with salt and pepper.
8. Grill the filets until desired doneness.
9. Place the warm corn mixture in center of each of 6 serving plates.
10. Top with a grilled filet.
11. Garnish with additional crumbled feta.
12. Serve immediately.

Wisconsin Buffalo Macaroni and Cheese Bites

Ingredients:

1 package (16 oz.) uncooked ditalini pasta
6 tbsps. butter, cubed and divided
2 garlic cloves, minced and divided
3/4 cup Panko bread crumbs
3 tbsps. minced fresh parsley, divided
3 tbsps. minced fresh dill, divided
1/4 cup all-purpose flour
1 cup milk
1/2 cup half-and-half cream
1/2 cup hot pepper sauce
2 tsps. ranch salad dressing mix, divided
1 cup. Mozzarella cheese, shredded
1 cup. sharp Cheddar cheese, shredded
Salt and pepper to taste
2 eggs, lightly beaten
2/3 cup crumbled Blue cheese
1 cup sour cream
1/3 cup buttermilk

Directions:

1. Heat oven to 350 degrees F.
2. Cook pasta according to package directions; drain.
3. Meanwhile, melt 2 tbsps. butter in a small skillet over medium-low heat.
4. Add 1 garlic clove; cook and stir for 1 minute.
5. Stir in Panko bread crumbs; toss to coat.
6. Remove from the heat.
7. Stir in 1 tbsp. each parsley and dill. Set aside.
8. Melt remaining butter in a Dutch oven over medium-low heat.
9. Whisk in flour until smooth.
10. Add remaining garlic clove; cook and stir for 1 minute.
11. Gradually whisk in milk, cream, hot pepper sauce and 1 tsp. ranch salad dressing mix.
12. Bring to a boil; cook and whisk for 2 minutes or until thickened.
13. Reduce heat to low; gradually stir in mozzarella and cheddar until melted.

14. Season with salt and pepper to taste.
15. Remove from the heat. Whisk a 1/4 cup hot cheese sauce into eggs in a bowl.
16. Return all to pan; whisk to combine.
17. Stir in pasta.
18. Divide pasta mixture into 48 greased mini muffin cups; press down gently.
19. Sprinkle with blue cheese and reserved bread crumb mixture.
20. Bake for 20-25 minutes or until a thermometer reads 160 degrees F and pasta is lightly brown and bubbly.
21. Let stand 10 minutes in pans before serving.
22. Combine sour cream with buttermilk.
23. Season with remaining parsley, dill and ranch salad dressing mix to taste.
24. Serve with mac and cheese bites.

Wisconsin Fondue

Ingredients:

1 large shallot, minced
2 tbsps. butter
2 garlic cloves, minced
1 cup lager or pilsner beer
4 cups (16 oz.) Wisconsin cheddar cheese, shredded
1 tbsp. flour
1 1/2 tsps. mustard powder
1/4 tsp. paprika
1/4 tsp. cayenne pepper
Salt and pepper to taste
Sliced apples, cubed jalapeno cheddar or French bread, broccoli and cauliflower florets for dipping

Directions:

1. Sauté shallot in butter in a small saucepan over medium-low heat until tender.
2. Add garlic; cook and stir 1 minute longer.
3. Stir in beer; heat until warm.
4. Reduce heat to low.
5. Toss cheddar with flour, mustard powder, paprika and cayenne pepper in a bowl.
6. Gradually add cheese mixture to saucepan, stirring constantly between each addition until melted.
7. Season with salt and pepper.
8. Transfer cheese sauce from the saucepan into a warm fondue pot.
9. Keep warm.
10. Serve with apples slices, jalapeno cheese or French bread cubes, broccoli and cauliflower florets.

Wisconsin Brie Torte

Ingredients:

12 oz. blue cheese crumbles
1 package (8 oz.) cream cheese
1 wheel (19.6 oz.) brie cheese
3/4 cup honey roasted pecan halves
1 cup dried cranberries
Assorted crackers

Directions:

1. Place blue cheese and cream cheese in a food processor; cover and process until combined.
2. Carefully slice brie horizontally into three disc-shaped portions.
3. Spread a third of the blue cheese mixture over the bottom portion.
4. Sprinkle with half of the pecans.
5. Top with brie.
6. Spread with a third of the blue cheese mixture.
7. Sprinkle with half of the cranberries.
8. Top with brie (rind side up).
9. Spread with remaining blue cheese mixture.
10. Sprinkle with remaining pecans and cranberries.
11. Cover and refrigerate for at least 1 hour.
12. Serve with crackers.

Wisconsin Pumpkin Pie Baked Brie

Ingredients:

1 wheel (8 oz.) Brie cheese
1 roll refrigerated pie crust dough
3 tbsps. pumpkin pie filling
2 tbsps. chopped pecans
1 tbsp. brown sugar
1 egg
1 tbsp. water
1 tbsp. sugar
Water crackers or fresh apple and pear slices

Directions:

1. Heat oven to 425 degrees F. Line a 15 x 10-inch baking sheet with parchment paper.
2. Trim rind from top of brie if desired; place in freezer for 10 minutes.
3. Unroll pie crust dough onto a lightly floured work surface; cut into 3/4-inch wide strips. Set aside.
4. Spread pumpkin pie filling over brie.
5. Sprinkle with pecans and brown sugar. Weave pie crust strips over the pecan topping creating a lattice, allowing excess dough to drape over the top and sides of cheese.
6. Gently tuck pie crust strips underneath brie to completely cover bottom, trimming if necessary for cheese to lay flat.
7. Place cheese on prepared pan. Whisk egg with water; brush over tops and sides of pie crust strips.
8. Sprinkle with sugar.
9. Bake for 12-15 minutes or until pie crust is golden brown and cheese is softened. Cool for 10 minutes before serving.
10. Serve with crackers or fresh fruit slices.

Wisconsin Cheesy Chicken Enchilada Dip

Ingredients:

1 medium onion, chopped
1 tbsp. butter
1 can (10 oz.) enchilada sauce
1 can (4 oz.) chopped green chilies
1 cup shredded cooked chicken breast
1-2 tsps. hot sauce, optional
1 pkg. (8 oz.) cream cheese, cut into small cubes
1 cup shredded Monterey jack cheese, divided
1 cup shredded mild cheddar cheese , divided
Sour cream
Chopped green onions
Tortilla chips

Directions:

1. Sauté onion in butter in a large, well-seasoned, cast-iron skillet or a large, oven-proof skillet over medium heat until crisp-tender, about 5 minutes.
2. Reduce heat; stir in enchilada sauce, green chilies, chicken and hot sauce if desired.
3. Bring to a gentle boil.
4. Reduce heat; simmer until sauce mixture is reduced by half, stirring constantly.
5. Remove from heat.
6. Whisk in cream cheese until melted.
7. Add 3/4 cup each Monterey jack and cheddar; stir to combine.
8. Sprinkle with remaining cheeses.
9. Broil 1-2 minutes or until the cheeses are melted (watch carefully). Garnish with sour cream and green onions.
10. Serve with tortilla chips.

Wisconsin Pepper Jack Pimento Cheese Spread

Ingredients:

1 1/2 cups (6 oz.) shredded pepper jack cheese
1/2 cup (2 oz.) shredded white cheddar cheese
4 oz. cream cheese, softened
1 jar (4 oz.) diced pimientos, drained
5 dill pickle slices
2 tbsps. dill pickle juice
1 tbsp. pickled jalapeño juice, optional
1 tbsp. mayonnaise
Toasted baguette slices or crackers

Directions:

1. Place the pepper jack, cheddar, cream cheese, pimientos, pickle slices, pickle juice, jalapeno juice if desired and mayonnaise in a food processor.
2. Cover and pulse until mixture is a spreadable consistency, about 5-10 pulses.
3. Spread on a toasted baguette slices or crackers.

Wisconsin Smoky Blue Cheese Bacon and Water Chestnut Dip

Ingredients:

6 strips thick-cut bacon
1/4 cup brown sugar, packed
1 tsp. cayenne pepper
1 pkg. (8 oz.) Wisconsin cream cheese
1/2 cup sour cream
1 can (8 oz.) diced water chestnuts, drained
1 cup (6 oz.) Wisconsin smoked blue cheese, crumbled*

Directions:

1. Heat oven to 350 degrees F.
2. Line baking sheet with foil and place wire cooling rack on top.
3. Lay strips of bacon on cooling rack. Rub brown sugar onto bacon strips; sprinkle with cayenne pepper.
4. Bake 15-20 minutes, or until bacon is cooked through, but not too crisp, and sugar is caramelized.
5. Remove from oven and cool. Chop bacon and set aside.
6. In bowl of electric mixer, combine cream cheese and sour cream until smooth.
7. Add chopped bacon, water chestnuts and crumbled smoked blue cheese; mix well to incorporate.
8. Dip may be served as is, or use a food processor to achieve a more consistent texture (pulse 4-5 times, do not over process).
9. Cover and chill 30 minutes before serving.
10. Serve with hearty crackers or crudité.

Wisconsin Spicy Cheesy Bratwurst Dip

Ingredients:

1/2 tbsp. extra-virgin olive oil
1/2 medium onion, diced
3 cooked bratwursts, chopped or cubed in bite-sized pieces
2 tbsps. jalapeños, diced
4 oz. Wisconsin cream cheese
1 heaping tbsp. Dijon mustard
3/4 cup sour cream
1/2 cup (2 oz.) Wisconsin cheddar cheese, shredded
3 cups (12 oz.) Wisconsin chipotle cheddar, shredded
1/2 cup cornichons or pickles, diced

Directions:

1. Heat oven to 350 degrees F. Heat olive oil in large non-stick pan over medium heat. After 1 minute, add diced onions and sauté for 3-4 minutes, or until tender. Adjust heat to medium low.
2. Add bratwurst, jalapeños and cream cheese.
3. Mix well.
4. Remove pan from heat and add Dijon mustard, sour cream, cheddar, chipotle cheddar and cornichons.
5. Mix until well combined.
6. Pour into 5x7-inch baking dish.
7. Bake 20 minutes, or until bubbly.
8. Remove from oven.
9. Heat broiler and place dip under, broiling 2 to 3 minutes, or until cheese topping is slightly browned.
10. Remove and serve immediately.

Wisconsin Roasted Brussels Sprout and Bacon Cheddar Dip

Ingredients:

2 cups Brussels sprouts, trimmed and halved
1 tbsp., plus
1 tsp. canola oil, divided
Salt to taste
1/4 cup onion, diced
1 clove garlic, minced
2 tbsps. mayonnaise
1/2 cup sour cream
8 oz. Wisconsin cream cheese
2 cups (8 oz.) Wisconsin sharp cheddar cheese, shredded
5 strips bacon, fried and crumbled plus additional for garnish, if desired

Directions:

1. Heat oven to 425 degrees F. Line baking sheet with parchment.
2. Toss Brussels sprouts with 1 tbsp. canola oil and pinch of salt.
3. Roast 15-20 minutes or until Brussels sprouts are tender and edges are brown and crisp.
4. Cool slightly.
5. Reduce oven heat to 400 degrees F.
6. While sprouts roast, cook onions and garlic in small sauté pan over medium heat with 1 tsp. canola oil and pinch of salt, until onions are soft and translucent, about 5 minutes.
7. Remove onions/garlic from pan and set aside to cool slightly.
8. In bowl, combine mayonnaise, sour cream, cream cheese and cheddar with roasted Brussels sprouts, onions and crumbled bacon.
9. Spoon mixture into baking dish and bake i5 minutes or until browned and bubbling.
10. Let dip rest at least 5 minutes before serving.
11. Garnish with additional bacon and Brussels sprouts, if desired.
12. Serve warm with toasted baguette slices or crackers.

Wisconsin Blue and Cheddar Beer Spread

Ingredients:

3 cups (12 oz.) Wisconsin cheddar cheese, shredded
2 cups (12 oz.) Wisconsin blue cheese, crumbled
1/3-1/2 cup wheat ale
Salt and black pepper to taste

Directions:

1. Mix cheeses and beer in food processor until thoroughly combined.
2. Add salt and black pepper to taste and additional beer for desired consistency.

Gnocchi and Triple Cheese

Ingredients:

2 pkgs. (16 oz. each) mini potato gnocchi
4 tbsps. truffle butter or butter, cubed and divided
3 tbsps. all-purpose flour
1 garlic clove, minced
2 cups milk
1 1/2 cups Swiss, shredded
1 cup Cheddar cheese, shredded
3/4 cup Parmesan cheese, grated and divided
1 tsp. kosher salt
1/2 tsp. pepper
1/4 cup unseasoned bread crumbs
1 tbsp. minced fresh parsley

Directions:

1. Heat oven to 375 degrees F.
2. Cook gnocchi according to package directions; drain and keep warm.
3. Melt 3 tbsps. butter in a Dutch oven over medium-low heat. Whisk in flour until light golden brown.
4. Add garlic; cook and stir for 1 minute.
5. Gradually whisk in milk.
6. Bring to a boil.
7. Cook and whisk for 2 minutes or until thickened.
8. Reduce heat to low; gradually stir in petite swiss, cheddar and ½ cup parmesan until melted.
9. Stir in gnocchi, salt and pepper.
10. Remove from the heat.
11. Spoon gnocchi mixture into a greased 8-inch baking dish.
12. Melt remaining butter in a bowl; toss with bread crumbs, parsley and remaining parmesan to coat.
13. Sprinkle bread crumb mixture over pasta.
14. Bake for 10-15 minutes or until topping is lightly browned and sauce is bubbly.
15. Let stand 5 minutes before serving.

Wisconsin Caramelized Onion Pasta Gratin

Ingredients:

3 pounds yellow onions, halved and thinly sliced
1/4 cup olive oil, divided
3/4 pound uncooked rigatoni pasta
3 tbsps. butter, cubed
1/4 cup all-purpose flour
1 cup milk
1 cup beef broth
2 1/2 cups Swiss cheese, shredded and divided
Salt and pepper to taste
2 slices white bread, torn into pieces
2 tbsps. fresh thyme leaves

Directions:

1. Sauté onions in 2 tbsps. olive oil in batches a Dutch oven until tender, adding more oil if necessary.
2. Reduce heat to medium-low.
3. Cook sautéed onions for 20-25 minutes or until golden brown, stirring occasionally.
4. Remove onions from pan when desired colored is reached; set aside.
5. Heat oven to 350 degrees F.
6. Cook pasta according to package directions until al dente; drain.
7. Set aside.
8. Melt butter in a Dutch oven over medium-low heat.
9. Whisk in flour until smooth.
10. Gradually whisk in milk and beef broth.
11. Bring to boil; cook and whisk for 2 minutes or until thickened.
12. Reduce heat to low; gradually stir in 1 cup of Swiss until melted.
13. Stir in reserved onions and pasta.
14. Remove from the heat.
15. Season with salt and pepper to taste.
16. Spoon pasta mixture into a greased 13 x 9-inch baking dish.
17. Place bread, thyme and remaining swiss in a food processor.
18. Cover and process until coarse crumbs.
19. Drizzle with remaining 2 tbsps. olive oil; toss to combine.
20. Sprinkle over pasta mixture.
21. Bake for 15-20 minutes or until crumbs are golden brown.

Wisconsin Three-Cheese Lasagna

Sauce Ingredients:

2 tbsps. olive oil
1 lb. bulk Italian sausage
1 lb. lean ground beef
1 large onion, chopped
3 cloves garlic, minced
1 tsp. dried basil
1 tsp. dried oregano
1/2 tsp. salt
1/4 tsp. black pepper
2 tbsps. tomato paste
1 can (28 oz.) crushed tomatoes
1 can (28 oz.) whole tomatoes

Filling Ingredients:

2 containers (16 oz. each) Wisconsin ricotta cheese
2 egg yolks
1 cup (4 oz.) Wisconsin parmesan cheese, grated
1 tsp. dried basil
1/2 tsp. salt
1/4 tsp. pepper
Olive oil or cooking spray
16 no-boil lasagna noodles
1 1/2 pounds Wisconsin fresh mozzarella, shredded*

Sauce Directions:

1. Heat olive oil in large Dutch oven or sauce pot over medium-high heat.
2. Add sausage.
3. Cook, breaking up sausage with wooden spoon, until browned and cooked through, about 8 minutes. Using slotted spoon, remove sausage and set aside.
4. Add ground beef and cook, breaking up with wooden spoon, 5 minutes.
5. Add onions.
6. Cook, stirring occasionally, until onions are translucent, about 6-7 minutes.
7. Add garlic and cook 1 minute.
8. Return reserved sausage to pot.
9. Add basil, oregano, salt, pepper and tomato paste.

10. Mix well and cook 1 minute.
11. Add crushed and whole tomatoes.
12. Bring to simmer and cook 5 minutes, breaking up whole tomatoes with spoon.
13. Adjust salt and pepper to taste.
14. Remove from heat and set aside.

Filling Directions:

1. In large bowl, combine ricotta and egg yolks.
2. Mix well.
3. Add parmesan, basil, salt and pepper.
4. Mix well to combine.

Assembly Directions:

1. Grease 9×13-inch casserole dish with olive oil or cooking spray.
2. Spread 2 cups sauce over bottom of pan.
3. Top with 4 lasagna noodles.
4. Spread 1/4 ricotta mixture over noodles.
5. Top with 3/4 cup mozzarella.
6. Repeat (sauce, noodles, ricotta mixture, mozzarella) 3 times, skipping mozzarella on 4th layer.
7. Top with 4 noodles, remaining sauce and remaining mozzarella.
8. Grease sheet aluminum foil with olive oil or cooking spray.
9. Cover lasagna loosely with foil.
10. Bake 45 minutes.
11. Remove foil and bake additional 25 minutes uncovered.
12. Let sit at least 10 minutes before serving.

Wisconsin Cheesy Manicotti Pasta Bake

Ingredients:

1 pound ground beef
1 small onion, chopped
2 cloves garlic, minced
3 cups water
1 package (16 oz.) medium shell pasta
1 can (14 oz.) crushed tomatoes
1 can (8 oz.) tomato sauce
1 tbsp. sugar
3/4 tsp. dried basil
1/2 tsp. dried Italian seasoning
Salt and black pepper to taste
1 cup (8 oz.) Wisconsin ricotta cheese
2 cups (8 oz.) Wisconsin mozzarella cheese, shredded
1 cup (4 oz.) Wisconsin parmesan cheese, shredded

Directions:

1. Heat oven to 475 degrees F.
2. In Dutch oven or large stock pot, brown beef and onion over medium heat, about 5 minutes.
3. Drain, leaving beef and onion in the pot.
4. Stir in garlic and simmer 30 seconds.
5. Add water, uncooked pasta, crushed tomatoes, tomato sauce, sugar, basil, Italian seasoning, salt and pepper.
6. Bring to boil, reduce heat; simmer, uncovered, until pasta is tender, about 15 minutes.
7. Season to taste with additional salt and pepper.
8. Drop large scoops of ricotta cheese on top of pasta.
9. Sprinkle with mozzarella and parmesan.
10. Bake until cheese is melted and bubbly, about 15-20 minutes.

Wisconsin Cheesy Spinach and Artichoke Pasta

Ingredients:

1 pound linguine (or pasta of your choice)
3 cups marinated artichoke hearts, drained and chopped (reserve marinating liquid)
3 cups baby spinach, coarsely chopped
1 cup Wisconsin parmesan cheese, freshly grated
1 cup Wisconsin mozzarella cheese, torn into small pieces
1/2 tsp. freshly ground black pepper

Directions:

1. Bring a large pot of generously salted water to a rolling boil.
2. Add the linguine and cook until al dente, approximately 8 minutes. Reserve approximately 1/2 cup of the pasta water and set aside.
3. Drain the pasta without rinsing.
4. Immediately transfer the linguine to a large bowl and add in 1 tbsp. reserved oil from the marinated artichokes along with the baby spinach.
5. Use tongs to toss the ingredients, allowing the heat from the pasta to wilt the spinach.
6. Once the spinach has wilted, stir in the artichoke hearts, parmesan cheese, mozzarella cheese, and pepper.
7. Add in the reserved pasta water as needed, sparingly, to keep the pasta from becoming sticky as the cheese absorbs up much of the moisture.
8. Taste for seasoning.
9. Add additional oil from the marinated artichokes jar if desired.

Wisconsin Tomato Corn Bake with Havarti

Ingredients:

2 ears fresh corn (1 1/2 cups kernels)
1 pint grape tomatoes, halved
2 tbsps. olive oil
2 cloves garlic, minced
1/3 cup mayonnaise
2 tbsps. fresh lemon juice
Salt and pepper, to taste
1 cup (4 oz.) Havarti cheese, grated
1-2 tbsps. fresh basil leaves, chopped

Directions:

1. Heat oven to 425 degrees F.
2. Cut corn kernels from cob.
3. Place corn and tomatoes in roasting pan, drizzle with olive oil and toss to coat.
4. Sprinkle with garlic.
5. Roast 20 to 25 minutes until beginning to brown, stirring occasionally.
6. Meanwhile in small bowl, combine mayonnaise, lemon juice, salt and pepper.
7. Remove corn mixture from oven and pour into a 1-quart casserole dish.
8. Add mayonnaise mixture, havarti and basil.
9. Return to oven to melt cheese, about 5 minutes.

Pasta with Wisconsin Sweet Corn Gremolata

Ingredients:

1 pound spaghetti
2 cups fresh sweet corn kernels, cooked
1/4 cup fresh basil, chopped
1/4 cup flat leaf parsley, chopped
1/4 cup extra virgin olive oil
Zest of 1 lemon, plus additional for serving
2 tbsps. lemon juice
2 garlic cloves, minced
Salt and pepper to taste
1 pint cherry tomatoes, halved
3 green onions, thinly sliced
1 cup (slight 4 oz.) Wisconsin parmesan cheese, grated, plus additional for serving

Directions:

1. Cook spaghetti al dente, according to package directions.
2. While pasta is cooking, mix together corn, basil, parsley, oil, lemon zest, lemon juice and garlic in medium bowl.
3. Season with salt and pepper.
4. Add tomatoes and green onions. Set aside.
5. Drain pasta and toss with corn mixture.
6. Add parmesan.
7. Adjust salt and pepper to taste.
8. Serve with additional parmesan and lemon zest.

Wisconsin BBQ Corn and Gouda Grilled Cheese

Ingredients:

4 oz. Wisconsin cream cheese, room temperature
3 tbsps. cilantro, chopped
2 ears corn, grilled and kernels cut from cob (1 1/2 cups)
Salt and pepper to taste
4 tbsps. barbecue sauce
8 1-oz. slices Wisconsin gouda cheese
1/2 small red onion, thinly sliced
4 tbsps. butter, softened
8 slices hearty white bread

Directions:

1. In small bowl, combine cream cheese, cilantro, corn, salt and pepper.
2. Stir to combine, then set aside.
3. Heat cast iron skillet or griddle over medium low heat.
4. Assemble sandwiches by spreading thin layer of barbecue sauce on 4 bread slices.
5. Top each with 1 slice gouda, cream cheese mixture, red onion, and a second slice of gouda. Top with remaining bread slices. Generously butter one side of sandwiches.
6. Place in skillet, butter-side-down. Butter remaining side.
7. Cook until cheese is slightly melted and bread is toasty and brown.
8. Flip sandwich and cook until cheese is completely melted.
9. Let sandwiches stand for 1 minute, and slice in half.

About the Author

Laura Sommers is **The Recipe Lady!**

She lives on a small farm in Baltimore County, Maryland and has a passion for food. She has taken cooking classes in Memphis, New Orleans and Washington DC. She has been a taste tester for a large spice company in Baltimore and written food reviews for several local papers. She loves writing cookbooks with the most delicious recipes to share her knowledge and love of cooking with the world.

Follow her on Pinterest:

http://pinterest.com/therecipelady1

Visit the Recipe Lady's blog for even more great recipes:

http://the-recipe-lady.blogspot.com/

Visit her Amazon Author Page to see her latest books:

amazon.com/author/laurasommers

Follow the Recipe Lady on Facebook:

https://www.facebook.com/therecipegirl

Follow her on Twitter:

https://twitter.com/TheRecipeLady1

Other Books by Laura Sommers

- Recipes for Chicken Wings
- 50 Super Awesome Salsa Recipes!
- Delicious Chip Dip Cookbook
- Authentic Traditional Memphis, Tennessee Recipes
- Traditional Kentucky Recipes
- Best Traditional Cajun and Creole Recipes from New Orleans
- 50 Super Awesome Coleslaw and Potato Salad Recipes

Made in the USA
Monee, IL
12 December 2024

73270343R00046